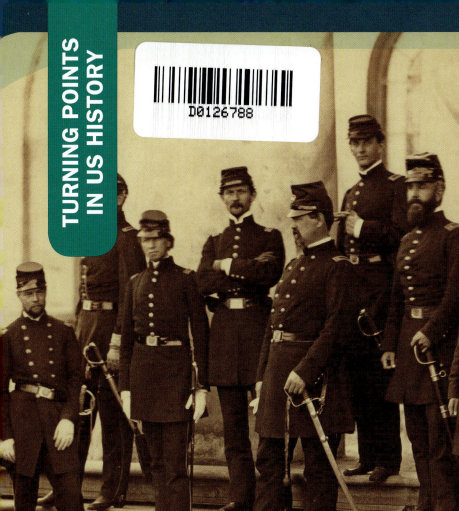

# 12 INCREDIBLE FACTS ABOUT THE
# US CIVIL WAR

by Robert Grayson

www.12StoryLibrary.com

12-Story Library is an imprint of Peterson Publishing Company and Press Room Editions.

Produced for 12-Story Library by Red Line Editorial

Photographs ©: Library of Congress, cover, 1, 8, 16, 18, 19, 20, 24, 25; Timothy H. O'Sullivan/Library of Congress, 4; Anthony Berger/Library of Congress, 5; Red Line Editorial/Rainer Lesniewski/Shutterstock Images, 6; Currier & Ives/Library of Congress, 9, 17; Bettmann/Corbis, 10, 27; Corbis, 12, 13, 23; Liljenquist Family Collection of Civil War Photographs/Library of Congress, 14, 28; William Horace Smith/Bettmann/Corbis, 15; Taylor & Huntington/Library of Congress, 21; traveler1116/iStockphoto, 22, 29; Coast-to-Coast/iStockphoto, 26

**ISBN**
978-1-63235-133-3 (hardcover)
978-1-63235-176-0 (paperback)
978-1-62143-228-9 (hosted ebook)

**Library of Congress Control Number: 2015934267**

Printed in the United States of America
Mankato, MN
June, 2015

12
STORY
LIBRARY

Go beyond the book. Get free, up-to-date content on this topic at 12StoryLibrary.com.

# TABLE OF CONTENTS

# SOUTHERN STATES FORM INDEPENDENT NATION

In the mid-1800s, most people in the United States could not imagine the nation splitting in two. Yet that was becoming a real possibility. Northern and Southern states disagreed about slavery. The South's economy was based on slavery.

Slaves were black people who had been kidnapped from Africa. They were brought to the United States to work. Slaves were forced to work without pay. But slavery was illegal in Northern states. For decades Northern states had been pushing

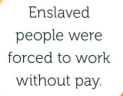

Enslaved people were forced to work without pay.

to make slavery illegal throughout the nation.

On November 6, 1860, Abraham Lincoln was elected president. Lincoln was a Northern Republican from Illinois. He didn't believe in slavery. Republicans wanted to ban slavery in any new US territory or state. But they would allow slavery to continue in the states that already had it. Lincoln agreed with this plan.

Southerners did not trust Lincoln. They believed he and his supporters would pass laws to end slavery. On December 20, 1860, South Carolina voted to secede, or break away from the nation. Six more Southern states followed: Alabama, Florida, Georgia, Louisiana, Mississippi, and Texas. Representatives of these seven states met on February 4, 1861. They formed a separate nation. They called it the Confederate States of America. They elected their own president, Jefferson Davis.

Lincoln took office as president of a divided nation on March 4, 1861. He declared that secession was illegal. He vowed to reunite the country.

Abraham Lincoln

## 7

**Number of states that left the Union before President Lincoln took office in 1861.**

- Slavery was legal in the South. It was illegal in the North.
- Southern states that left the Union created their own nation. It was called the Confederate States of America.
- Lincoln vowed to reunite the country.

5

# US ARMY OFFICERS RESIGN TO JOIN THE CONFEDERACY

On April 12, 1861, Confederate troops launched an attack on Fort Sumter in South Carolina. Fort Sumter was a military fort in the middle of Charleston Harbor. It belonged to the US government. After two days of fighting, the fort's federal troops surrendered. The US Civil War had officially begun. Now

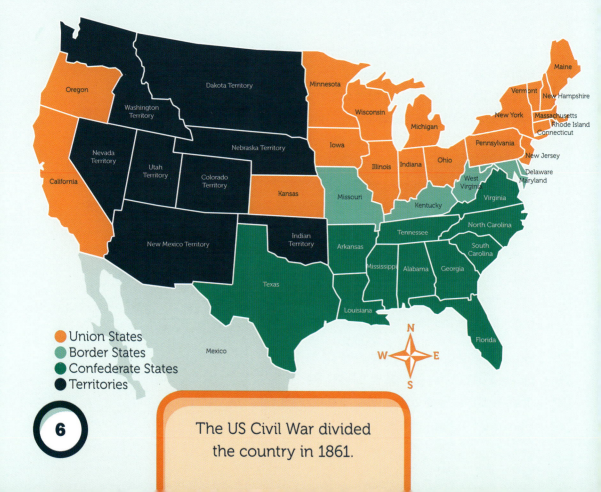

- ● Union States
- ● Border States
- ● Confederate States
- ● Territories

The US Civil War divided the country in 1861.

generals in the US Army had to pick a side.

Lincoln responded to the Fort Sumter attack. He called up 75,000 volunteer troops. These troops would protect the United States, or the Union, from the Confederacy. Each state still in the Union had to supply troops. But some Southern states did not want to fight against their Southern neighbors. Arkansas, North Carolina, Tennessee, and Virginia seceded from the Union. They joined the Confederacy.

Virginia was home to many of the finest military men in the US Army. One of these men was Robert E. Lee, a colonel. He had served for 32 years. But when Virginia seceded, Lee resigned from the US Army. He joined the Confederate Army, as a major general, to protect his home state. Other military men, including Thomas Jonathan "Stonewall" Jackson, James Ewell Brown "Jeb" Stuart, and Joseph Eggleston Johnson, followed suit.

# 300
### Approximate number of US Army officers who resigned to fight for the Confederacy.

- The remaining states in the United States were called the Union.
- Lincoln called up 75,000 volunteer troops to protect the Union.
- Some Southern officers did not want to fight against their home states. Many left the US Army and joined the Confederate Army.

## BORDER STATES

Not all Southern states that allowed slavery seceded. Delaware, Kentucky, Maryland, Missouri, and West Virginia were slave states that remained in the Union. They were called border states because they made up the border between the warring sides. Some people in the border states agreed with the Confederacy. Others supported the Union.

# EARLY CONFEDERATE VICTORIES STUN UNION FORCES

As the US Civil War began in 1861, the Confederates showed their strength early. On July 21, 1861, they beat Union forces at the First Battle of Bull Run in Virginia. It was the first major battle of the war. Union troops were surprised by the South's strength. The Union was forced to retreat.

As the first year of the war passed, the Confederate victories continued in the southeast. Confederate General Jackson bulldozed through northwest Virginia's Shenandoah Valley between March and June 1862.

First Battle of Bull Run

The South was victorious in the Second Battle of Bull Run.

Then Southern forces fought back Union troops as they tried to capture Richmond, Virginia. Called the Seven Days' Battles, these battles stretched from June 25 to July 1, 1862. The Confederacy also defeated the Union in the Second Battle of Bull Run on August 29 and 30, 1862.

Meanwhile, Union troops were winning more battles in the southwest. The Union hoped to divide its troops to the east and the west of the South. They wanted to conquer the South from all sides. But in the early months of the war, they struggled to gain ground.

## 4,878
### Estimated number of casualties on both sides in the First Battle of Bull Run.

- The Confederacy won early battles in the eastern part of the country.
- The Union was surprised by the Confederacy's strength in battle.
- The Union hoped to divide its troops and conquer the South from all sides.

# WOMEN CHARGE INTO BATTLE DISGUISED AS MEN

On September 17, 1862, Union Private Franklin Thompson was looking for wounded soldiers. The Battle of Antietam in Sharpsburg, Maryland, had just ended. With a combined death toll of 3,650,

Sarah Edmonds disguised herself as a man to fight for the Union.

**THINK ABOUT IT**

Why do you think neither army allowed women to join its ranks? Make a list of your reasons.

# 400

Approximate number of women who fought in the US Civil War.

- Women were not allowed to join the Union or Confederate armies.
- Some women disguised themselves as men to enlist.
- If a woman was discovered in the ranks, she was sent home.

it was the bloodiest single day of the war so far. Thompson found a young soldier, severely wounded. Thompson called over a surgeon. But he said he could do nothing to save the soldier's life. The doctor left.

The dying soldier then told Thompson that he was actually a woman. She had disguised herself as a man. She had wanted to fight alongside her brother for the Union. The soldier asked Thompson not to reveal her secret. Thompson completely understood because Thompson was also a woman. Franklin Thompson was really Sarah Edmonds from Flint, Michigan. She enlisted on May 25, 1861. She wanted to help save the Union by fighting in the war.

When the war broke out, some women wanted to fight just as men did. But neither the Union nor the Confederacy allowed women to serve. Hundreds of women disguised themselves as men. They cut their hair and put on men's clothing. Then they enlisted in the army.

Female soldiers usually went unnoticed unless they were wounded or someone from their hometown recognized them. If discovered, the women were sent home. But many women fought without their true identity being revealed. Some even rose through the ranks without detection.

# WAR INTRODUCES NEW MILITARY TECHNOLOGY

War often spurs the invention of new technology. Each side wants to have the upper hand on its enemy. So each side works to invent new war technologies. The US Civil War prompted the development of many innovations.

Mass-produced canned food came on the scene for the first time in the Civil War. Tin cans kept food fresh longer. They made it easier to feed an army on the move.

Gas-filled and hot-air balloons allowed armies to spy from the air. This was the first airborne technology used in war. Men flew in two-foot-high (0.6-m) wicker baskets hanging from the balloons. They reported troop movements with flag signals.

Later in the war, troops used telegraphs for communication. Telegraphs made it possible for Abraham Lincoln to contact his generals on the battlefield. The North was much more advanced in telegraph technology than the South. It had the upper hand when it came to communication.

Newly developed railroads helped troops and supplies move quickly. Again, the North had the big

Men prepare a hot-air balloon for launch.

Gatling gun

## THINK ABOUT IT

Research the different inventions developed during the war. Write a paragraph about which one you think is the most important and why.

advantage. It had three times as much track as the South. Almost all the train factories were located in the North too.

Rapid-fire weapons also made an impact. These were pistols and rifles that could fire more than one shot before being reloaded. The Gatling gun was developed near the end of the war. It was the forerunner to the modern-day machine gun. It could fire hundreds of rounds a minute.

## WAR PHOTOGRAPHY

The Civil War marked the first time a war was covered extensively through the lens of a camera. Photography had been invented just prior to the war. Taking pictures was a complex process. It required chemicals and heavy equipment. This made it difficult to take photos of combat. Instead, portraits and post-battle photographs told the story of the war.

# 200

Number of rounds per minute the Gatling gun could fire.

- The wartime needs of armies prompted innovations.
- Telegraphs and railroads helped spread news and resources quickly.
- Rapid-fire weapons made warfare even more deadly.

13

# FREED SLAVES JOIN UNION ARMY

On September 22, 1862, President Abraham Lincoln issued the Emancipation Proclamation. This document freed all slaves in seceded states that did not return to the Union by January 1, 1863. None of the states returned to the Union by the deadline. In eyes of the US government, slaves in those states were free. But the Union did not have control over the Southern states. It could not enforce the new rule.

An African-American Union soldier in uniform

The Union also now permitted former slaves to join the army. Casualties on both sides in the Civil War were enormous. The Union's ranks got a big boost when African-American men began enlisting in 1863.

When the war first broke out in 1861, thousands of African-American men tried to enlist in the Union Army. But they could not join. A law passed in 1792 prevented it. In 1862, new laws allowed free African Americans to enlist. That,

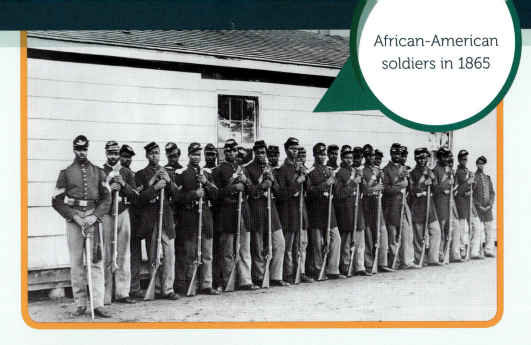

African-American soldiers in 1865

# 200,000

**Approximate number of African-American soldiers who served in the Union Army.**

- Many African Americans enlisted in 1863.
- A combination of the Emancipation Proclamation and changes to laws in the Union allowed freed slaves to join the Union Army.
- African-American soldiers were discriminated against, given lower pay than white soldiers, and segregated from white soldiers.

combined with the Emancipation Proclamation, prompted thousands of African-American men to join the Union Army.

Many African-American soldiers suffered prejudice in the army. African-American soldiers earned less money than white soldiers. They were put in segregated regiments.

By the end of the war, hundreds of thousands of African Americans had served. They made up 10 percent of the Union Army. Thousands more served in the Union Navy. Roughly 38,000 African-American soldiers died in the war.

# 7

## GENERAL "STONEWALL" JACKSON IS ACCIDENTALLY SHOT

The smoke had barely cleared after the First Battle of Bull Run on July 21, 1861, and General Thomas Jonathan Jackson was already a legend. During that battle, the Confederates were struggling. As Confederate generals tried to rally their troops, Jackson stood up on the battlefield. He was waiting for the next burst of Union fire. His men stood up with him. Southern General Barnard Bee yelled to his men, "Look! There is Jackson standing like a stone wall! Rally behind the Virginians!" The Confederates did. They fought off the Union forces to claim victory. After that, Jackson was known as "Stonewall." He led his men to many victories. But he would meet a tragic end.

On May 2, 1863, Jackson launched several surprise attacks against the Union in the Battle of Chancellorsville in Virginia. Hundreds of soldiers fell on both sides. But Jackson's troops' attacks on the Union Army were the most devastating.

As night fell on May 2, Jackson wanted to continue the attack. He scouted out Union positions on horseback.

General "Stonewall" Jackson

Then he rode back to the Confederate lines. With tensions high, stressed young Southern soldiers mistook Jackson for an enemy soldier. They opened fire, wounding the general. Jackson was carried from the scene for medical aid. But he ordered his men to continue to fight.

Jackson's wounds were severe. His left arm had to be amputated. But doctors felt he would recover. However, eight days later the general died of pneumonia. It was a complication of the surgery. Jackson's death was one of the most devastating losses the Confederacy suffered.

Jackson died after being wounded on the battlefield.

# 3

## Number of times Jackson was shot by his own men.

- Jackson was one of the Confederate Army's top leaders.
- In the dark, he was mistaken for an enemy soldier.
- The most severe wound was in Jackson's left arm.

# VICTORIES HELP THE UNION

The Confederacy did not feel it was necessary to win the war. Southern leaders believed that if they could drag the war on, they could wear down the North. That would force Abraham Lincoln to negotiate a peace treaty that would favor the South. They had many early victories. But things started to change in July 1863. The North won two battles that changed the course of the war. This eventually spelled disaster for the Confederacy.

Between July 1 and 3, 1863, the deadliest battle of the war was fought in Gettysburg, Pennsylvania. Led by General Robert E. Lee, the Confederate Army hoped to push into the North. They wanted to move the fighting out of the South. But after three days of combat, Lee's army had to retreat. More than 51,000 soldiers were killed, wounded, or captured in the battle. The battle ended when the Confederates retreated back through Maryland to Virginia.

Meanwhile, Union General Ulysses S. Grant beat back Confederate forces in Vicksburg, Mississippi.

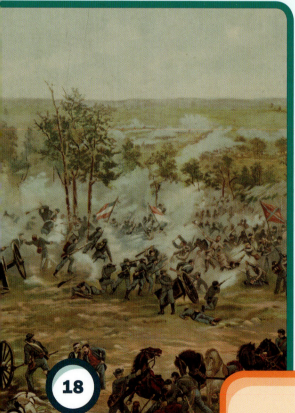

The Battle of Gettysburg

The victory came on July 4, 1863. There were approximately 19,000 casualties on both sides. This gave the Union control of the Mississippi River. By controlling the river, the Union split western and eastern Confederate forces in half.

Ulysses S. Grant led Union forces in the Battle of Vicksburg.

## 70,233
### Estimated combined casualties from the Gettysburg and Vicksburg battles.

- Union victories at Gettysburg and Vicksburg were the turning point of the Civil War.
- The Union's victory at Gettysburg stopped the Confederates' push northward.
- The victory at Vicksburg gave the Union control of the Mississippi River.

## DOGGED DETERMINATION

Sallie, a brindle bull terrier, was the mascot of the 11th Pennsylvania Volunteer Infantry Regiment. She had been in battles with her unit since 1862. In the confusion of the Battle of Gettysburg, Sallie got separated from her unit. She could not be found for three days. When the fighting ended, she was discovered standing watch over the dead and wounded from her unit.

# SHERMAN'S MARCH TO THE SEA DESTROYS THE SOUTH

By 1864, the Confederates were running out of resources to fight the war. Yet they refused to give up. Union leaders decided that the only way to the defeat the South was to destroy it. Union General William Tecumseh Sherman was charged with this mission.

Sherman left Chattanooga, Tennessee with 100,000 soldiers on May 4, 1864. He was heading to Atlanta, Georgia,

General William Tecumseh Sherman

## FEARLESS COMMANDER

William Tecumseh Sherman was born in Lancaster, Ohio, in 1820. He attended the US Military Academy at West Point. He served in the US Army from 1840 to 1853. He left to become a banker. In 1859, Sherman took a position as a school superintendent in Louisiana. He returned to the US military in 1861, when war seemed unavoidable.

135 miles (217 km) away. Along the route, his troops smashed through any Confederate troops they found. They took control of Southern territory as they traveled. On September 2, 1864, Sherman's troops captured Atlanta, Georgia. This was the South's last major transportation center. It was a huge victory.

In November 1864, Lincoln won a second term as president. Shortly

Sherman's troops destroyed railroad tracks in the South.

after this, Sherman's troops left Atlanta. They headed to the seaport city of Savannah, Georgia. His men destroyed everything in their path. This became known as Sherman's March to the Sea.

Sherman's troops were ruthless. They destroyed private homes and possessions and burned crops. They took whatever they needed on their way to Savannah. Southerners were stunned.

When Sherman arrived in Savannah on December 21, 1864, he rested for a short time. Then, in January 1865, Sherman and his troops carried their campaign through South Carolina and kept going north. It would take decades for the South to recover from the damage done by Sherman's army.

## 285

Distance, in miles (459 km), from Atlanta to Savannah in Sherman's March to the Sea.

- Sherman's army devastated the South and broke the spirit of the Confederacy.
- The troops left nothing in their wake.
- Private homes and property were destroyed.

# AS CONFEDERATES SURRENDER, UNION TROOPS SALUTE

In March 1865, Union Army Commander-in-Chief Ulysses S. Grant knew his troops were closing in on the Confederate Army. On April 2, 1865, Confederate troops fled Richmond, Virginia, the Confederate capital. The Union Army seized control of the city.

Led by General Robert E. Lee, the Confederates retreated until Union forces surrounded them in the village of Appomattox Court House, Virginia. Lee's army was outnumbered. They were critically low on supplies, especially food. The Confederate general had no options left. He had to discuss terms of surrender with Grant.

On April 9, 1865, the two generals met. Grant offered generous terms. The Confederates had to turn over their weapons. Confederate soldiers were allowed to return home. They could take their horses and mules

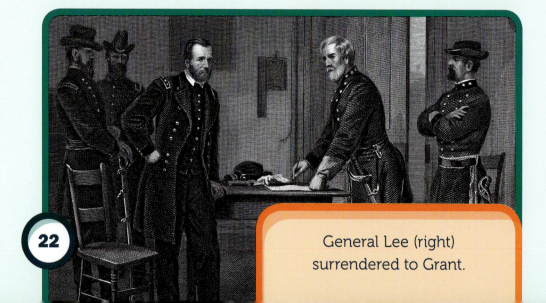

General Lee (right) surrendered to Grant.

## THINK ABOUT IT

Imagine that you are either a Union or a Confederate soldier at the surrender ceremony. Write a paragraph about how you would feel after watching former enemies salute each other.

# 15,000

Approximate number of Confederate troops under Lee's command who surrendered at Appomattox Court House.

- Confederate soldiers were allowed to return home.
- Soldiers could keep their mules and horses.
- Both sides saluted each other at the surrender ceremony.

with them. "The war is over," said Grant. "The Rebels are our countrymen again."

At 5:00 a.m. on April 12, 1865, Confederate troops marched into Appomattox Court House. Led by General John B. Gordon, the troops formally surrendered. They were surrounded by Union troops, under the command of

General Joshua Lawrence Chamberlain.

Chamberlain ordered his men to "shoulder arms" as a salute to the Confederates. Gordon, on horseback, turned toward Chamberlain. Gordon commanded his horse to bow his head. And he ordered his men to return the salute. Gordon would later comment that the scene was "a token of respect from Americans to Americans."

Chamberlain had his Union soldiers salute their former enemies.

# CASUALTIES MAKE CIVIL WAR BLOODIEST CONFLICT

At the end of the Civil War in 1865, 620,000 were estimated dead as a result of the war. It was roughly 2 percent of the US population. In today's terms, that would equal 6 million people. Newer estimates, released in 2012, put the figure closer to 750,000 lives lost. Either way, the Civil War is the nation's bloodiest conflict.

Some of the casualty figures were shocking. For example, the University of Mississippi had a student body of 139. Almost all of them, 135, enlisted in Company A of the 11th Mississippi Infantry. All were either killed or wounded at Gettysburg.

The dead were difficult to identify. The military did not use dog tags yet. Some troops wrote their names on their clothes. That way, they could be identified if they died in battle. Oftentimes, bodies of soldiers went unidentified. They were buried with no markers.

Because of simple medical practices at the time, many soldiers died of battlefield wounds. In the mid-1800s, there were no antibiotics

A Union Army hospital in Washington, DC

24

Surgeons in front of a hospital tent

and no vaccines. Surgery was performed wherever doctors could find room, including in schoolhouses and barns and on the battlefield. Many soldiers died from infections after surgery.

Many more soldiers died of disease. For every three soldiers killed in action, five died of disease. Soldiers died of typhoid, dysentery, pneumonia, malaria, smallpox, tuberculosis, and measles.

# 1.5 million

Estimated total number of Civil War dead, wounded, captured, or missing.

- Between 620,000 and 750,000 soldiers are believed to have died in the Civil War.
- Hundreds of thousands died from noncombat-related diseases.
- Many soldiers died from infections after surgery.

## OTHER CASUALTIES

In addition to those dead, many soldiers were severely wounded, captured, or reported missing. In the Civil War, there were approximately 400,000 soldiers wounded. Another 476,000 soldiers were estimated captured or listed as missing.

# LINCOLN BECOMES ONE OF THE WAR'S LAST VICTIMS

On the night of April 14, 1865, just days after the Confederates had surrendered at Appomattox Court House, President Abraham Lincoln was watching a play at Ford's Theatre in Washington, DC. After 10,000 battles, the Civil War was coming to an end. But there would be one more victim.

As the second scene of the third act of the play began, a shot rang out. Lincoln slumped over in his chair. John Wilkes Booth, a Confederate sympathizer, had shot the president in the head. Booth had snuck into the balcony where the president was sitting. After shooting Lincoln, Booth jumped from the balcony to the stage. He escaped.

Ford's Theatre still stands.

An army surgeon rushed to Lincoln's side. But he said the president would not survive. Lincoln died the next morning at 7:22 a.m. The Union Army conducted a manhunt for Booth. They trailed him to a barn in Virginia. The troops killed Booth during a gunfight on April 26, 1865.

As the war-torn country worked to reunite, it would have to do so without Lincoln. The South, left in ruins after the war, needed to rebuild. It also needed to adjust to a way of life that was not based on the free labor of slaves. Former slaves struggled to find justice in a country still steeped in racism. For them, the end of the Civil War was the beginning of a battle for equal rights.

## 9

**Number of hours Lincoln lived after being shot.**

- Lincoln was killed by Southerner John Wilkes Booth.
- Booth was killed 12 days later by federal troops.
- After the Civil War, freed slaves would have to fight for equal rights.

Newly freed slaves in the South

# 12 KEY DATES

**November 6, 1860**
Abraham Lincoln is elected president of the United States.

**December 20, 1860**
South Carolina becomes the first state to secede from the Union.

**April 12, 1861**
Southern troops launch an attack on Fort Sumter, starting the Civil War.

**July 21, 1861**
The Confederacy wins the first true battle of the war at the First Battle of Bull Run.

**August 29–30, 1862**
The Confederacy beats back the Union at the Second Battle of Bull Run.

**January 1, 1863**
The Emancipation Proclamation takes effect.

**May 2, 1863**
Confederate General "Stonewall" Jackson is accidentally shot by his own men.

**July 1–3, 1863**
The Union triumphs at the Battle of Gettysburg.

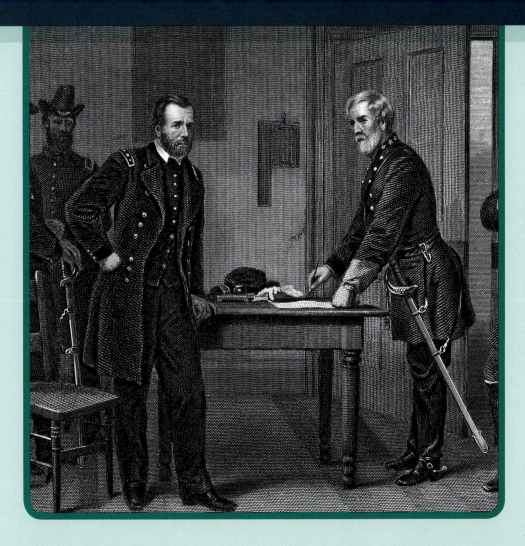

### July 4, 1863
Victory at the Battle of Vicksburg gives the Union control of the Mississippi River.

### November 1864
Union General William Tecumseh Sherman begins his March to the Sea.

### April 9, 1865
The Confederacy surrenders at Appomattox Court House, Virginia, ending the Civil War.

### April 14, 1865
President Abraham Lincoln is assassinated.

# GLOSSARY

**amputate**
To cut off a limb, such as an arm or a leg.

**campaign**
A series of military moves to achieve a goal.

**casualty**
A soldier who is wounded, dead, or reported missing during combat.

**dog tag**
A small, thin piece of metal, engraved with a soldier's identification information, and worn around the neck.

**emancipation**
The act of freeing a person from slavery.

**innovation**
Something new, such as an invention.

**prejudice**
An opinion based on assumptions rather than fact.

**regiment**
A unit of an army.

**secession**
The act of separating from a larger entity, such as the United States.

**segregated**
Separated based on a person's race.

# FOR MORE INFORMATION

## Books

Kent, Zachary. *The Civil War: From Fort Sumter to Appomattox.* Berkeley Heights, NJ: Enslow, 2011.

Martin, Iain C. *Gettysburg: The True Account of Two Young Heroes in the Greatest Battle of the Civil War.* New York: Sky Pony Press, 2013.

Stanchak, John. *Eyewitness Civil War.* New York: DK Publishing, 2011.

## Websites

### Civil War Trust
www.civilwar.org/education/students/kidswebsites.html

### National Geographic: Top Ten Civil War Sites
travel.nationalgeographic.com/travel/top-10/civil-war-sites

### US National Park Service: The Civil War
www.nps.gov/civilwar/index.htm

# INDEX

## About the Author

Robert Grayson is an award-winning former daily newspaper reporter and the author of books for young adults. Throughout his journalism career, Grayson has written stories on historic events, sports figures, arts and entertainment, business, and pets.

## READ MORE FROM 12-STORY LIBRARY

Every 12-Story Library book is available in many formats, including Amazon Kindle and Apple iBooks. For more information, visit your device's store or 12StoryLibrary.com.